D0269213

# BANKSY

## Art Breaks the Rules!

First published in 2014 by Wayland

Copyright © Wayland 2014

Wayland
338 Euston Road
London
NW1 3BH

Wayland Australia
Level 17/207 Kent Street
Sydney NSW 2000

Senior editor: Julia Adams

Produced for Wayland by Dynamo
Written by Hettie Bingham

Picture acknowledgements:
**Key: b=bottom, t=top, r=right, l=left, m=middle, bgd=background**

**Alamy** p17 mr Stefano Baldini; p19 tr Cathy DeWitt **REX** p12 tr Adrian
Sherratt;
p14 mr Rex; p15 m Sipa Press; **Shutterstock** Backgrounds and Doodles:
Pixotico; Edvard Moinar; Banana Republic Images; Mike McDonald;
Apartment; GreenBelka; schab; Prapann; Alexandra Dzh; Larysa Ray;
Butenkov Aleksei; McLura. p1 m, p19 b BMCL; p6 bl, p30 tr 1000 words; p22
tr 360b; p23 br anderm; p8 br, p9 bl, p10 tr, p11 tr, p13 bl, p27 m, p29 br
ChrisDorney; p7 tr David Fowler; p24 m Donald Bowers Photography; p23 tr
Frank Wasserfuehrer; p16 m Jeremy Reddington; p20 tr, p21 br Padmayogini;
p2 tr, p18 br Radoslaw Lecyk; p4/5 m Yoann MORIN

Dewey classification: 759.2-dc23
ISBN 978 0 7502 8265 9
E-book ISBN 987 0 7502 8780 7

Printed in China
10 9 8 7 6 5 4 3 2 1

Wayland is a division of Hachette Children's Books,
an Hachette UK company.
www.hachette.co.uk

CONTENTS

# BANKSY

# WHO IS BANKSY?

Who exactly is Banksy? His identity is a closely-guarded secret, but we're pretty sure that he's a man and it is thought he comes from Bristol. We don't know his real name, his exact age or anything about his family...

There are some things we do know about Banksy, though. We know about some of his opinions, his original sense of humour and his unique perspective on life. These are things we can learn about him through his art.

Banksy's art is public. He draws on walls because he wants the world to see and understand his perspective on life. His art can have a funny message or a serious one, but all his works are designed to make us think and to look at life from a different angle.

'A LOT OF PEOPLE NEVER USE THEIR INITIATIVE BECAUSE NO ONE TOLD THEM TO.'

BANKSY

'ART SHOULD COMFORT THE DISTURBED AND DISTURB THE COMFORTABLE.'

BANKSY

'ALL ARTISTS ARE PREPARED TO SUFFER FOR THEIR WORK, BUT WHY ARE SO FEW PREPARED TO LEARN TO DRAW?'

BANKSY

Grafitti art by Banksy in Passage Du Moulin Des Pres, October, 2012

## They seek him here, they seek him there...

Banksy has given very few interviews to journalists over the years (and with no guarantee that it really was him), but he has never allowed his photograph to be taken. On the rare occasions he has been filmed, he was heavily disguised. Only a few trusted friends know his true identity. Bansky has revealed that even his parents didn't know who he was – they thought he was a painter and decorator. Perhaps they still do!

'THERE ARE NO EXCEPTIONS TO THE RULE THAT EVERYONE THINKS THEY'RE AN EXCEPTION TO THE RULES'
BANKSY

'IT DOESN'T TAKE MUCH TO BE A SUCCESSFUL ARTIST – ALL YOU NEED TO DO IS DEDICATE YOUR ENTIRE LIFE TO IT. THE THING PEOPLE MOST ADMIRED ABOUT PABLO PICASSO WASN'T HIS WORK/LIFE BALANCE.'

BANKSY

# EARLY WORK

During the 1990s, the city of Bristol was establishing an underground culture of street art and graffiti that continues to this day. Back then, it was claimed that Banksy was part of a Bristol graffiti crew known as DryBreadZ (DBZ). Now he is one of the world's most famous contemporary artists.

Inspired by the graffiti artist 3D, who formed the music group Massive Attack, Banksy started making graffiti in the classic New York style with big, spray-painted letters. In a rare interview he admits that he was never very good at working in that style because it took him too long to do. He needed to come up with a way to produce his work more quickly; he was worried he would get caught by the police, because what he was doing was against the law. Eventually Banksy decided he could work more quickly using stencils and has been using this technique since around the year 2000.

Banksy's work began to appear in Bristol and London. Around this time, Banksy met Steve Lazarides, a photographer turned art dealer, who began selling Banksy's work and later became his agent. Steve worked with Banksy until 2009, when the pair parted company for reasons unknown.

This graffiti piece in Bristol by Banksy prompted Bristol City Council to ask the public whether graffiti should be left or removed.

A mural by Banksy on the seafront at St.Leonards-on-Sea, East Sussex – August, 2010

## They seek him here, they seek him there...

Banksy has never been caught in the act of creating his work. Some of his earliest pieces have been painted over or removed. Some people now regret that because Banksy's work sells for a great deal of money these days!

'I CAME FROM A RELATIVELY SMALL CITY IN SOUTHERN ENGLAND. WHEN I WAS ABOUT TEN YEARS OLD, A KID CALLED 3D WAS PAINTING THE STREETS HARD. I THINK HE'D BEEN TO NEW YORK AND WAS THE FIRST TO BRING SPRAY PAINTING BACK TO BRISTOL. I GREW UP SEEING SPRAY PAINT ON THE STREETS WAY BEFORE I EVER SAW IT IN A MAGAZINE OR ON A COMPUTER.'

BANKSY

# IS IT ART?

Art critics and the public are divided when it comes to Banksy's status as an artist. Some think he is a vandal, but many think he is a genius. There are fans of his work all around the world and his style is mimicked everywhere. His designs can be found on T-shirts, calendars and even cushion covers – much the same as Van Gogh's famous *Sunflowers*, for instance. Banksy's work is now more commonly found in art galleries than on a brick wall and it sells for large amounts of money when it comes up at auction.

Islington Council in North London spends a great deal of money removing illegal graffiti. However, it has taken the view that Banksy's work is public art and it sees it as a gift. It never removes work that is thought to be by Banksy.

Banksy's 'Sunflower', located in Bethnal Green, London – November 2007

'TO ME THERE'S NOTHING AT ALL INTERESTING ABOUT BANKSY... WHEN I SAW H[IS] STUFF AROUND I THOUGHT, "WELL, THAT'S AN ENTERTAINING BIT OF RUBBISH ON THE WALL." BUT NOW I'M SUPPOSED TO TAKE ALL THIS STUFF SERIOUSLY AND I DON'T REALLY KNOW WHAT I'M SUPPOSED TO SAY; IT'S QUITE OBVIOUS THAT HE ISN'T REALLY ANYTHING.'

**– MATTHEW COLLINGS, ART CRITIC**

'ART HAS ALWAYS BEEN INTERESTED IN REBELS... [BANKSY'S WORK] IS TYPICAL SUBVERSIVE ART BEHAVIOUR, IT'S WHAT ART DOES; IT GETS UP THE NOSES OF THE ESTABLISHMENT.'

**– WALDEMAR JANUSZCZAK, ART CRITIC**

'GRAFFITI DOES RUIN PEOPLE'S PROPERTY AND IS A SIGN OF DECAY AND LOSS OF CONTROL... RUNNING UP TO SOMEBODY'S PROPERTY OR PUBLIC PROPERTY AND DEFACING IT IS NOT MY DEFINITION OF ART. OR IT MAY BE ART BUT IT SHOULD NOT BE PERMITTED.'

**– MICHAEL BLOOMBERG, FORMER MAYOR OF NEW YORK**

'BANKSY IS... ALWAYS TOTALLY INVENTIVE AND NEW AND FRESH... I THINK FOR ANY ARTIST THAT'S REALLY RARE.'

**– DAMIEN HIRST, ARTIST**

# IS IT LEGAL?

**P**utting graffiti on a wall that doesn't belong to you is against the law in the UK under the Criminal Damage Act, 1971. Graffiti is seen by many as a public nuisance and is often associated with gang culture and anti-social behaviour.

Banksy's 'Pensioner Thugs' in London – December 2007.

**G**raffiti can be defined as drawings, scribbles, messages or tags that are painted, written, sprayed or etched onto walls or other surfaces. Anyone convicted of creating graffiti in the UK can be imprisoned, fined or ordered to do community service, depending on how much damage has been caused. However, there are ways of making street art that is legal. Some councils and private businesses provide special walls or structures for people to decorate with graffiti so that street artists are able to showcase their work.

**T**here is no doubt that some of Banksy's work has been carried out illegally. He keeps his identity such a closely guarded secret because he knows that if the police caught him he would be prosecuted.

# GETTING NOTICED

Once he had established his distinctive stencil style of graffiti in 2000, Banksy spent the next few years coming up with original ideas for his art. His pieces became a familiar sight on city streets – not just in London and Bristol but as far afield as Los Angeles, USA and Palestine in the Middle East. If people didn't yet know his name, they were certainly getting to know his work.

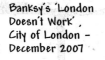

Banksy's 'London Doesn't Work', City of London – December 2007

**B**anksy's work began to attract the attention of the media, and the public began to look out for his stencils, waiting to see what would come next. He didn't disappoint; along came pictures of kissing policemen, rats holding placards, monkeys with weapons of mass destruction and the characters from the film *Pulp Fiction* holding bananas instead of guns.

# They seek him here, they seek him there...

Deciding to take his work further afield in 2002, Banksy took his street art to the 33⅓ Gallery in Los Angeles, USA, where he put on a show entitled Existencilism. This is a combination of the words 'stencil' and 'existentialism'. He also paid a visit to Sydney and Melbourne in Australia, where he left some of his trademark rats as a calling card.

Sometimes Banksy has painted slogans appearing like official notices. At various well-known landmarks he has stencilled 'This is not a photo opportunity'; elsewhere he has stencilled 'By Order of the National Highways Agency this Wall is a designated graffiti area'. These signs often remained for some time before anyone noticed that they had not been put there by city councils.

Banksy's 'One Nation Under CCTV', Oxford Street, London – June 2008

'THE PEOPLE WHO TRULY DEFACE OUR NEIGHBOURHOODS ARE THE COMPANIES THAT RAWL GIANT SLOGANS ACROSS BUILDINGS AND USES, TRYING TO MAKE US FEEL INADEQUATE UNLESS WE BUY THEIR STUFF.'
BANKSY

As Banksy's fame grew, his work began to appear in places other than on the street. In 2003, the pop group Blur asked him to design the cover of their album, Think Tank. Banksy doesn't usually take on commercial work but explained, 'I've done a few things to pay the bills, and I did the Blur album. It was a good record and [the pay was] quite a lot of money.' The artwork from the album cover sold at auction for £75,000 in 2007.

# BANKSY AND

In 2003, Banksy hit the headlines when he displayed a piece of his work in an art gallery – but his painting didn't get there in the usual way.

**B**anksy came up with an idea he believed nobody had tried before – adding graffiti to classically-styled oil paintings. To establish the idea as his own, Banksy decided that his work should appear in a famous art gallery. He wasn't expecting an invitation any time soon, so he took matters into his own hands. Heavily disguised, he took a piece of his work into Tate Britain, a gallery in London, and simply stuck it on the wall himself when nobody was looking.

**T**he picture was of an idyllic country scene to which he had added a stencil of police tape, the kind used to cordon off a crime scene. He put a label next to the work which read: (Banksy 1975). Crimewatch UK Has Ruined The Countryside For All Of Us. 2003. Oil On Canvas.

The painting was only discovered when it crashed to the floor a few hours later. His act, however short lived, led to mass exposure for Banksy and his work, as the story was covered on national news.

# TATE BRITAIN

Painting in the style of Degas with an image of Simon Cowell

## They seek him here, they seek him there...

Banksy put another version of the painting he left at Tate Britain up for sale in London's Tom Tom gallery, along with a video of himself secretly hanging the painting in the Tate Britain.

I n a witty response, Tate Britain issued a statement saying that a 'man had left a personal possession in one of the galleries' and that it was 'currently being held in lost property'.

'IT WAS FUNNY; I WAS GOING INTO ALL THESE GALLERIES BUT I WASN'T LOOKING AT THE ART; I WAS LOOKING AT THE BLANK SPACES.'

BANKSY

B anksy went on to add a few more of his own masterpieces to vacant spaces in art galleries, including a copy of Leonardo Da Vinci's famous *Mona Lisa* holding a bazooka rocket.

# EXHIBITIONS

In 2003, Banksy decided the time was right to hold an exhibition of his work, but he doesn't really like art galleries, so he put on a show in his own distinctive way.

**R**enting a massive warehouse, Banksy put together his Turf Wars exhibition. The show ran for five days in East London. It was no ordinary show. His exhibits featured live animals that were painted in various ways, one example being a cow covered in images of Andy Warhol's face. The

animals he used were all show animals and used to being on public view. The paint was animal-friendly too. The RSPCA said that the conditions were good enough, but some animal rights campaigners didn't agree – one person chained themselves to some nearby railings to protest.

'A PART OF ME WISHES I COULD GO [TO THE TURF WARS EXHIBITION] BECAUSE I'VE PUT TOGETHER A REALLY NICE SETUP.'
BANKSY

**B**anksy also held a 12-day exhibition in London's Westbourne Grove in 2005. This featured classic paintings with some of his distinctive added touches – such as Monet's famous water lily pond to which he added an abandoned shopping trolley.

**B**arely Legal was an exhibition put on by Banksy in 2006, this time in Los Angeles, USA. Once again the show featured painted live animals. The star of the show was an elephant painted pink and gold to match the wallpaper which it stood in front of. Many people thought this symbolized the idea that we sometimes don't see what's right in front of us.

**V**illage Pet Store and Charcoal Grill was Banksy's first official exhibition in New York, held during 2008. The show included moving puppets of a chicken watching over little chicken nuggets as they pecked away at a packet of barbeque sauce.

**I**n the summer of 2009, people queued for hours to see Banksy's Summer Exhibition in Bristol – the city it is thought he comes from. The exhibition was held at the Bristol City Museum and Art Gallery and featured over one hundred of his works, many of which were new. His art was displayed in and amongst the museum's regular exhibits.

# CONTROVERSIA

**Banksy's art always has something to say. His messages can be humorous or political – and often both. He expresses himself in a way that gets noticed.**

The massive concrete wall separating Israel from the Palestinian territories proved too much of a temptation for Banksy to resist in 2005. The Israeli authorities say that they built the wall to protect Israel from suicide bombers, but the United Nations has declared the wall illegal. With a statement on his website saying that he believes the wall 'essentially turns Palestine into the world's largest open prison,' Banksy set off to express his views on the subject through his art.

## WHAT ARE YOU LOOKING AT?

He created nine murals on the wall, each sending a subtle message to the world. One showed a silhouette of a girl floating up holding onto a bunch of balloons. Another showed comfortable-looking armchairs by a window with a beautiful view through it.

'A WALL HAS ALWAYS BEEN THE BEST PLACE TO PUBLISH YOUR WORK.'
BANKSY

# THEMES

Guantanamo Bay is an American prison for suspected terrorists in Cuba. Some people believe that the people held there may be a threat to security, but others think that the prison should be closed and that the prisoners held there should be either charged with a crime or released. To make people think about the issue, in 2006 Banksy dressed an inflatable doll in orange overalls to look like a Guantanamo prisoner, then placed the doll in Disneyland, California.

In 2004, for the seventh anniversary of Princess Diana's death, Banksy printed some mock £10 notes with her face on them instead of the Queen's. On the fake money was written: 'Bansky of England. I promise to pay the bearer on demand the ultimate price.' Take a look at a real £10 note to see what is actually written on it.

'IF YOU WANT TO SAY SOMETHING AND HAVE PEOPLE LISTEN THEN YOU HAVE TO WEAR A MASK. IF YOU WANT TO BE HONEST THEN YOU HAVE TO LIVE A LIE.'
BANKSY

'THE GREATEST CRIMES IN THE WORLD ARE NOT COMMITTED BY PEOPLE BREAKING THE RULES BUT BY PEOPLE FOLLOWING THE RULES. IT'S PEOPLE WHO FOLLOW ORDERS THAT DROP BOMBS AND MASSACRE VILLAGES.'
BANKSY

During the London Olympics in 2012, Banksy painted some controversial images onto walls and put photographs of them on his website. One mural showed an athlete throwing a javelin shaped like a missile. Another showed an athlete pole-vaulting over a fence onto a dirty old mattress.

# BANKSY'S MOST FAMOUS WORKS

**Banksy's distinctively styled satirical stencils are known the world over. There are some themes and images that he has created repeatedly over the years, which have become particularly famous.**

B anksy's monkeys are more than a little cheeky. Often they display messages on sandwich boards. Sometimes they pose as the Queen of England and occasionally they are even in possession of explosives!

R ats have always been a big favourite with Banksy, perhaps because they are rarely seen, even though they exist in their millions as a part of city life – rather like the millions of people who feel that they are not heard in modern life. Sometimes wearing necklaces, often holding a placard, many times with a camera: the Banksy rat is a creature of mischief.

**B**alloons make a frequent appearance in Banksy's work too, carrying people to freedom or just floating up and away...

**L**ittle girls are another popular subject in Banksy's art – a picture of innocence in a sometimes cruel world.

**P**olicemen are a common sight on city streets, partly thanks to Banksy's many pictures of them, often in unlikely poses (see below)!

BY ORDER
NATIONAL HIGHWAYS AGENCY
THIS WALL IS A DESIGNATED
GRAFFITI AREA
PLEASE TAKE YOUR LITTER HOME
EC RCF UMDA 33/300

# EXIT
# THROUGH

When Banksy turned his hand to film-making, the result was an award-winning documentary. Premiered at the Sundance Film Festival in the USA, his film raised more questions than it answered and caused quite a stir.

Exit Through the Gift Shop is a movie directed by Banksy and released in 2010. Filmed as a documentary, it is about Thierry Guetta, a Frenchman living in Los Angeles, who is obsessed with filming street artists at work. Although Thierry had wanted to film Banksy more than any other street artist, Banksy decided that Thierry was an interesting character, and made his own movie about him. Banksy suggested to Thierry that he could become a street artist himself and so, taking his advice, he reinvented himself as Mr. Brainwash, or MBW for short. MBW is now a successful artist and his work sells for high prices.

Street art by Mr Brainwash outside The Old Sorting Office, London, venue for his first solo show – September, 2012

'IT'S BASICALLY THE STORY OF HOW ONE MAN SET OUT TO FILM THE UN-FILMABLE. AND FAILED.'
– BANKSY

# THE GIFT SHOP

**B**anksy's film was nominated for quite a few awards, including an Oscar for 'Best Documentary' and a BAFTA for 'Outstanding Debut by a British Writer, Director or Producer'. He won 'Best Documentary' at the Austin Film Critics Award and an Eddie (American Cinema Editors Award) for 'Best Edited Documentary'.

When hearing of his Oscar nomination, Bansky said:

'THIS IS A BIG SURPRISE... I DON'T AGREE WITH THE CONCEPT OF AWARD CEREMONIES, BUT I'M PREPARED TO MAKE AN EXCEPTION FOR THE ONES I'M NOMINATED FOR.'

## They seek him here, they seek him there...

Because MBW's art was very similar to Banksy's own style, many people thought that the film was a hoax and that MBW was actually Banksy in disguise. Others thought that MBW was an actor; a living piece of art rather than a genuine character. Banksy, who doesn't usually confirm or deny any rumours, insisted that it was all true. Whichever version is true, the film was a success and won many awards.

Another controvesial piece of street art by Mr Brainwash (aka Thierry Guetta) at his first UK solo show – September, 2012

# BANKSY'S BOOKS

Banksy produced his work in a more conventional format when he wrote and published a series which he refers to as his 'three little books'.

**B**anging Your Head Against a Brick Wall was published in 2001, Existencilism followed in 2002 and Cut It Out was published in 2004. The three little titles were published by Banksy's imprint, Weapons of Mass Distraction. The books contain photos of his work and his thoughts about them.

Much street art is produced by unknown street artists. Banksy featured images like these in his book *Pictures of Walls* (below and top right).

'A WALL IS A VERY BIG WEAPON. IT'S ONE OF THE NASTIEST THINGS YOU CAN HIT SOMEONE WITH.'
– BANKSY

'A LOT OF MOTHERS WILL DO ANYTHING FOR THEIR CHILDREN, EXCEPT LET THEM BE THEMSELVES.'
– BANKSY,

In 2005, Banksy's 'three little books' were combined to create one title called *Wall and Piece*. In addition to reproducing images from his three previous books, *Wall and Piece* included some new material. Published by an established publisher, the book graced the shelves of high street retailers, placing his work next to titles from the conventional art world. The book was, and continues to be, a best seller in the art category.

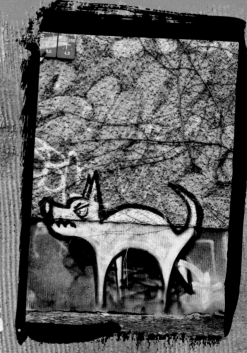

Banksy went on to compile and publish *Pictures of Walls* in 2005. This is a compilation of amusing art put on walls by street artists other than himself.

# BETTER OUT THAN IN

During October 2013, Banksy put on an outdoor art show on the streets of New York. His aim was to create a new piece of art for every day of October. Banksy promised:

'A UNIQUE KIND OF ART SHOW...'

It featured, in Banksy's words, 'elaborate graffiti, large scale street sculpture, video installations, and substandard performance art'. In a newspaper interview which took place via email, so that he could remain anonymous, Banksy explained:

'THE PLAN IS TO LIVE HERE, REACT TO THINGS, SEE THE SIGHTS – AND PAINT ON THEM. SOME OF IT WILL BE PRETTY ELABORATE, AND SOME WILL JUST BE A SCRAWL ON A TOILET WALL.'

When asked the reason for the show, he said:

'THERE IS ABSOLUTELY NO REASON FOR DOING THIS SHOW AT ALL.'

Banksy's show aimed to turn the city into a giant treasure hunt. Spotting his work was difficult though, because it sometimes disappeared as quickly as it had appeared, either being drawn over by other graffiti artists or removed by the authorities. The show also featured installations. In one piece, a truck covered in graffiti contained a scene of virtual paradise, complete with a waterfall.

## They seek him here, they seek him there...

Banksy set up a stall selling original pieces of his work for $60 on the streets of New York. The lucky few who bought paintings now own work that would sell for thousands of dollars, but most people just walked straight past.

For the duration of the show, Banksy communicated his ideas to the public through his website. He also posted a video installation on his website. The show came complete with a phone number providing a guided tour of his pieces around the city. The recording was styled as a mock version of audio tours commonly found in museums and galleries.

'NEW YORK CALLS TO GRAFFITI WRITERS LIKE A DIRTY OLD LIGHTHOUSE. WE ALL WANT TO PROVE OURSELVES HERE. I CHOSE IT FOR THE HIGH FOOT TRAFFIC AND THE AMOUNT OF HIDING PLACES. MAYBE I SHOULD BE SOMEWHERE MORE RELEVANT, LIKE BEIJING OR MOSCOW, BUT THE PIZZA ISN'T AS GOOD.'

Another truck, usually used to transport farm animals, roamed the streets of New York containing happy-looking puppet animals. There was even some performance art, where a fibreglass model of Ronald McDonald had his big clown-shoes polished by an actor dressed as an urchin.

# BANKSY'S CRITICS

**Many people admire Banksy, but not everyone is a fan. He has almost as many critics as he has admirers – some from the authorities and, surprisingly, some from other graffiti artists.**

While Banksy's street art is often protected by perspex guards and sought out by curious tourists, some people take a different view of his work. Tower Hamlets Council in London has decided to treat his work as vandalism. It has removed any Banksy art that has appeared and will continue to do so. A statement said:

'TOWER HAMLETS COUNCIL TAKES THE CLEANLINESS OF THE BOROUGH VERY SERIOUSLY AND IS COMMITTED TO REMOVING ALL GRAFFITI AS SOON AS POSSIBLE.'

It went on to explain that many of their residents think graffiti is an eyesore, saying that it makes their neighbourhoods feel less safe. It also costs thousands of pounds every year to clean it up.

Fellow street artists have been known to criticize Banksy too. Some reject his use of stencils, saying that his work is not true graffiti. They have also criticized him for becoming a 'sell-out', now that he has become famous and his work sells for high prices. During his street show in New York, Banksy's website featured a FAQ section which included the question: 'Why are you such a sell out?' and the answer: 'I wish I had a pound for every time someone asked me that.'

'I USED TO THINK OTHER GRAFFITI WRITERS HATED ME BECAUSE I USED STENCILS, BUT THEY JUST HATE ME.'
— BANKSY

'WE NEED TO BE CLEAR
HERE, GRAFFITI IS
A CRIME.'
– TOWER HAMLETS
COUNCIL

Banksy graffiti in Turnpike
Lane, London. The iconic
artwork was removed from
this wall to go on sale.

# ARE YOU BEST MATES WITH...

# BANKSY

By now you should know lots of things about Banksy. Test your knowledge of him by answering these questions:

**1** Which city is Banksy thought to have grown up in?

a) New York
b) London
c) Bristol

**2** What is Banksy's favourite type of rodent to draw?

a) Rats
b) Hamsters
c) Squirrels

**3** In which city was the exhibition Barely Legal held?

a) New York
b) London
c) Los Angeles

**4** For which band did Banksy design an album cover?

a) Oasis
b) Blur
c) West LIfe

**5** In which area of London was Turf Wars held?

a) North West London
b) South East London
c) East London

**6** In which London gallery did Banksy first leave a graffitied oil painting?

a) Tate Britain
b) Tate Modern
c) National Gallery

7 In which American city did Banksy put on Better Out Than In?

   a) Boston
   b) New York
   c) Chicago

8 What was the title of Banksy's 2010 film?

   a) Close the Door on your Way Out
   b) Exit Through the Gift Shop
   c) I Want my Money Back

9 By which graffiti artist was Banksy first inspired?

   a) 3D
   b) WD40
   c) 5P

10 What is the title of Banksy's best-selling book

   a) Far and Wide
   b) Wall and Piece
   c) Near and Far

Stencil graffiti piece by Banksy on a building on Mission Street in San Francisco, USA, circa May 2010.

# ANSWERS

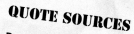

1  c) Bristol
2  a) Rats
3  c) Los Angeles
4  b) Blur
5  c) East London
6  a) Tate Britain
7  b) New York
8  b) *Exit Through the Gift Shop*
9  a) 3D
10  b) *Wall and Piece*

You can occasionally find out more information about Banksy by logging onto www.banksy.co.uk. A single tweet from the unverified Twitter account @banksy reads: BANKSY IS NOT ON TWITTER, however, by using #banksy you may find some interesting tweets.

## QUOTE SOURCES

**Page 4** Wall and Piece, 2006; **Page 5** Wall and Piece, 2006; **Page 7** B Movie (Banksy), 2010; **Page 8** B Movie (Banksy), 2010; **Page 11** Wall and Piece, 2006; **Page 13** B Movie (Banksy), 2010; **Page 14** The Guardian, 2003; **Page 16** Wall and Piece, 2006; **Page 17** Wall and Piece, 2006; **Page 20** The Guardian, 2010, Exit Through the Gift Shop, 2010; **Page 22** Wall and Piece, 2006; **Page 24** The Village Voice, 2013; **Page 25** The Village Voice, 2013; **Page 26** The Village Voice 2013 Wall and Piece, 2006;

## YOU CAN READ MORE ABOUT BANKSY IN THE FOLLOWING BOOKS:

*Banksy: The Man Behind the Wall*, by Will Elsworth-Jones (Aurum Press Limited, 2012)

*Banksy: You Are an Acceptable Level of Threat and if You Were Not You Would Know About It*, by Gary Shove (Carpet Bombing Culture, 2012)

*Banksy Myths & Legends*, by Marc Leverton (Carpet Bombing Culture, 2012)

## BANKSY HAS WRITTEN THE FOLLOWING BOOKS:

*Wall and Piece* (The Random House Group, 2005)

*Pictures of Walls*, conceived and compiled by Banksy (Picturesofwalls Limited, 2005)

# GLOSSARY

**Andy Warhol**
A 20th century American artist who led the pop art movement

**Blur**
A British rock band at their peak of fame in the 1990s

**Commercial**
Designed to make a profit

**Community service**
An activity carried out for the public good without pay, often ordered instead of a prison sentence or fine in a court of law

**Controversial**
Likely to cause disagreement and debate

**Crimewatch UK**
A BBC TV programme appealing for the public's help in solving crimes

**Idyllic**
A scene that is happy, peaceful and picturesque

**Inadequate**
Falling short of required standard

**Initiative**
The ability to make decisions and take actions on your own

**Leonardo da Vinci**
A famous 15th century Italian artist

**Massive Attack**
A British music group from Bristol

**Monet**
A famous 19th century French artist

**Mural**
A painting on a wall

**Picasso**
A famous 20th century Spanish artist

**Placard**
A board that is held up to display a slogan or message

***Pulp Fiction***
An American crime film directed by Quentin Tarantino, released in 1994

**RSPCA**
Royal Society for the Prevention of Cruelty to Animals

**Stencil**
A card with sections cut out to paint through, creating a pre-designed picture

**Subversive**
Seeking to disrupt an established system

**Tag**
A nickname or a particular mark used as the signature by a graffiti artist

**Vandal**
A person who deliberately damages property belonging to others

# INDEX